IN AN UNGUARDED MOMENT

IN AN UNGUARDED MOMENT

HANNY MICHAELIS
SELECTED POEMS

*Translated from the Dutch
by Judith Wilkinson*

Shoestring Press

All rights reserved. No part of this work covered by the copyright herein may be reproduced or used in any means – graphic, electronic, or mechanical, including copying, recording, taping, or information storage and retrieval systems – without written permission of the publisher.

Printed by imprintdigital
Upton Pyne, Exeter
www.digital.imprint.co.uk

Typesetting and cover design by The Book Typesetters
us@thebooktypesetters.com
07422 598 168
www.thebooktypesetters.com

Published by Shoestring Press
19 Devonshire Avenue, Beeston, Nottingham, NG9 1BS
(0115) 925 1827
www.shoestringpress.co.uk

First published 2022

© Copyright: Judith Wilkinson

© Cover portrait of Hanny Michaelis in conté by Eva Spakman (www.evy-kunstart.com), specially commissioned for this book

© Photograph of portrait by Michael Wilkinson

The moral right of the author has been asserted.

ISBN 978-1-915553-12-6

**Nederlands letterenfonds
dutch foundation
for literature**

Shoestring Press gratefully acknowledges the support of the Dutch Foundation for Literature.

ACKNOWLEDGEMENTS

Translations in this collection, or earlier versions of these translations, have appeared in the following publications: *Acumen, Dutch, De Hoffeskrant, Illuminations, Oasis, Orbis, Poetry Salzburg Review, The Enchanting Verses Literary Review* (India 2017), *Staying Human* (Bloodaxe, 2020), www.poetryinternational.org and www.languageandculture.net.

I would like to thank Anthony Runia for his invaluable suggestions; I am grateful to my late mother, Han Wilkinson-Dekhuijzen, for her feedback; and I am indebted to Rob Bartelds for his help with biographical research.

I would like to thank the Dutch Foundation for Literature for providing a translation grant.

Thanks are also due to Hanny Michaelis' publisher, Uitgeverij Van Oorschot, for permission to print these translations. The Dutch source texts are from her collected poems: Hanny Michaelis, *Verzamelde gedichten*, Van Oorschot, Amsterdam 2011.

CONTENTS

Introduction   1

SHORT PRELUDE (1949)
The Sunken Cathedral   11
Children's Corner   12
Ghetto Children   13
Farewell to Amsterdam   14

WATER OUT OF THE ROCK (1957)
The sky has the pallor   17
This is the hour when I don't want to be alone   18
Moving through time, we carefully   19
You took the blood-red route   20
This evening when I'd fled   21
Beyond each other's reach   22
Beneath restless clouds   23
You give me water   24
Listening to the music   25
Cold and infertile   26
Sleepless in the cavern   27
In October the light   28

AGAINST THE WIND (1962)
What did you do   31
You: a deposed tyrant   32
Abandoned   33
Underwater   34
Invisibly   35
Slowly I move on   36
Years later   37
Give me the elusive oasis   38
With her Egyptian eyes   39
Somewhere in this city   40
The night is lighter   41
In an unguarded moment   42
Ominously low   43
If it isn't ours   44

Thinking of how we used to be together 45
Submerged 46
Footsteps coming down the stairs. 47
Taste me 48
Sad 49
In the leafless light 50
Disconcertingly close-to-the-bone 51

UNEXPECTED (1966)
Tantalising uncertainty 55
Minutes spread 56
It's terrible 57
Intimacy 58
When the inexpressible 59
Midnight. Moon 60
Some days I see gems 61
The racket of an alarm clock 62
The I who 63
Love rolled away 64
Over the years 65
On a country road 66

THE ROCK OF GIBRALTAR (1969)
This evening I learnt 69
In the dead of night 70
It's an ordinary day. The sun 71
Three floors up in the heart 72
Irretrievably buried 73
Sparrows twittering 74
In the light 75
The suppressed glow 76
Late in the afternoon 77
Distant lightning 78
The body 79
A hilltop under majestic 80
An elongated factory 81
I was about three years old 82
Philosophising brilliantly 83
A body trusted and familiar 84

RUSHING HEADLONG TOWARDS A NEW UTOPIA (1971)

Reaching the bars of her cage	87
Five o'clock on a Saturday afternoon	88
A day out had brought us	89
Stretched out on your back	90
What it would have been like	91
Five identical tower blocks	92
Statements	93
Not the chord stretched to	94
Faces in a haze	95
Chattering away and full of purpose	96
When, with light fingertips	97
He who closes his curtains	98
Your face unrecognisably	99
A morning	100

POEMS PUBLISHED POSTHUMOUSLY

How charmingly	103
The white, brazen stare	104
Slowly but surely	105
Suddenly, from somewhere	106
As dusk was setting in	107
I don't want to be grateful and make do	108
The smoke of my cigarette	109
That evening I waited for a long while	110
Deep into the evening	111
Indestructible. A word	112
The night after I learnt	113
A ruinous wind	114
Today and yesterday	115

Notes 116

INTRODUCTION

Hanny Michaelis is known in the Netherlands for her epigrammatic precision and quiet lyricism, a lyricism tempered by an almost wry awareness of limitation. Her harrowing experiences during World War II, and the struggles she had during her life, undoubtedly account for the mournful note in much of her poetry.

Michaelis was born in 1922 in Amsterdam, the only child of liberal, non-religious Jews. Her father, who came from Germany, was an erudite, cultured man who had trained as a pianist at the Conservatorium in Berlin until his studies were cut short, due to his father's financial problems. He was sensitive, witty, an avid reader, but also unworldly and insecure. Michaelis' mother, who was four years older than her husband, was an intelligent, emancipated woman, and unconventional, like her husband. She worked as a bookkeeper and trade correspondent at an import-export firm and eventually became the family's sole breadwinner. When the crisis came in the 1930s, she lost her job, and the family had to rely on financial assistance from others. The marriage was reasonably happy, despite worries and quarrels about money.

Michaelis was closest to her father, with whom she shared her artistic sensibilities and musicality. She too was insecure, though she had inherited some of her mother's toughness and directness; she was undiplomatic, with a strong sense of justice, and she could be sharp.

Michaelis already wrote poems during her primary school days, and in the last two years of her grammar school she started writing sonnets. She was a voracious reader, and from the age of fourteen she began to read all the books in the house, from emigrant literature to psychology. Stefan Zweig, Joseph Roth, Kafka, Dickens, Thomas Mann and Freud were some of the writers whose work she explored. She also read a great deal of Dutch poetry. Among her favourites were Vestdijk, Slauerhoff and Marsman; the latter's highly visual poems about the Dutch landscape resonated with her. Even as a schoolgirl, she was a perceptive critic. Of Emily Dickinson she said: 'She is far ahead of her time and stands outside any fashion.' Of the Dutch novelist Anthony Donkers' work she wrote in her diary: 'You need more than humanity to write a good novel.' After the war, Anne Frank's father showed her his daughter's still-unpublished manuscript, and she instantly recognised its importance.

When the Occupation started in September 1939, the anti-Jewish measures didn't take effect straightaway; it wasn't until September 1941 that Jews had to wear a star. Michaelis was able to finish her school education. She very much wanted to go on to university to study Dutch literature, but Jews weren't allowed to attend further education or vocational courses. The family needed money, but there weren't many options, since Jews could not be employed by non-Jews. Michaelis ended up working as a home help in a Jewish family. During this time she continued to write poems.

In July 1942 Michaelis received a letter ordering her to report to the Gestapo. Fortunately, friends found a hiding-place for her straightaway; she had to pack some belongings quickly and was given the address to go to. The only books she took with her were Marsman's collected poems and some of Du Perron's collections. Her poem 'Farewell to Amsterdam' is about her departure that day.

Michaelis remained in hiding until the end of the war. During these difficult and lonely years, she was moved from one address to another whenever there was a risk of her hiding-place being betrayed. Some families treated her warmly, others exploited her and had her take care of all the cooking and cleaning. Many of her hosts were Dutch Reformed people, whose rigid beliefs were alien to hers. In her journal she wrote: 'I am trapped in a narrow Dutch Reformed circle, while more than ever I am becoming aware of my deep affinity with socialism and communism.' And yet she was also appreciative of the kindness she often received, and she kept in touch with some of her hosts after the war.

Although she was occasionally able to go outside, in part because she didn't look Jewish, she was still confined to her room much of the time and had to keep away from windows. Throughout these years she continued to keep a journal and write poetry; a number of the poems from her first collection,

Klein voorspel ('Short Prelude'), were written during this time. In March 1943 her parents, with whom she had stayed in touch by letter, were deported to the Dutch transit camp of Westerbork. Michaelis received their poignant last letter, thrown across the barriers and forwarded by a student. In it her parents expressed their love and their hopes of a reunion in calm and reassuring language. Long after the end of the war Michaelis found out through the Red Cross that her parents had been deported to Sobibor and gassed there.

When the war ended, Michaelis had nothing: no place to stay, no family. She got a job at Volksherstel, an aid organisation that helped people whose lives had been damaged by the war. She began to suffer bouts of depression that were to recur throughout her life.

Her next job was as a secretary at Meulenhoff publishers, where she began to meet other writers. In 1946 she met the novelist Gerard Reve at Meulenhoff's, and later that year they met again, at an award ceremony, when Reve received a prize for his famous novel *De avonden* ('The Evenings'). Reve was a complicated man, handsome, challenging and unconventional; Michaelis was beautiful, witty and fiery, but timid too. She had already published poems in various journals when they met. They soon moved in together and in 1948 got married. Like her mother, Michaelis became the main breadwinner, as Reve initially earned little from his writing. The marriage was difficult from the start, as it soon became clear that Reve was more interested in men, and he began to have lovers. Despite the rows they had, Michaelis was in many ways very tolerant, but eventually she began to distance herself and see other people. By then she had published her first collection, *Klein voorspel* ('Short Prelude'), which was well received by the press, and she was becoming more independent. She had left Meulenhoff and was working as a secretary for *Nieuw Israelietisch Weekblad*, a cultural journal aimed at the Dutch-Jewish community.

Reve frequently travelled abroad, but for a long while Michaelis was unable to join him, as her passport said 'stateless, formerly German', which made it hard for her to get a visa. It was not until 1951 that she acquired the Dutch nationality. What is striking is that, for a long time, both Reve and Michaelis tried to save their marriage, as the bond between them was in many respects strong. Michaelis never regretted the marriage and always remained a staunch supporter of Reve's work.

Reve began to visit London regularly, where he had fallen in love with James Holmes, a poet and translator, and from time to time Michaelis was able to visit him there. In 1955 she began a relationship with businessman Meik de Swaan, and yet her marriage to Reve still continued, with each leaving the other free. However, the problems between them were taking their toll on Michaelis, and she began to suffer from writer's block.

In 1957 Michaelis left her job at *Nieuw Israelietisch Weekblad* for a part-time position as a policy staff member for the Arts Department of the municipality of Amsterdam, where she was to work until 1984. In her spare time she continued to write poetry, as well as writing essays and reviews and translating children's books from French, German and English.

Reve, meanwhile, was still in London, and upon his return, he and Michaelis decided to separate, though it was not until 1959 that they were officially divorced. Michaelis' relationship with de Swaan lasted for two years, until he was killed in a plane crash. After that she had no other long-term relationships.

She continued working for the Arts Department and was also on the board of various cultural organisations. In addition, she was a jury member for various literary awards, and through this work she met and befriended many other artists.

1957 was also the year in which Michaelis published her second collection, *Water uit de rots* ('Water out of the Rock'), which consolidated her reputation as a poet of note. Her fourth collection, *Onvoorzien* ('Unforeseen'), published in 1966, was awarded the prestigious Jan Campert Prize, and in 1995 she won two oeuvre prizes, the Sjoerd Leikeprijs and the Anna Bijns Prijs. In total she published six collections, and in 1989 Van Oorschot published a first Selected Poems, *Het onkruid van de twijfel* ('The Weeds of Doubt'). In 1996 a Collected Poems was published, which saw five reprints, and in 2005 the well-known Dutch novelist Voskuil published his own selection of her work.

In her later years Michaelis did not write much poetry, though in 2002, with the help of literary biographer Nop Maas, she did produce a memoir, *Verst verleden* ('Most Distant Past'), focusing on her youth and her time in hiding during the war. She also translated some Hebrew and Yiddish poetry late in life. Increasingly, however, she retreated from public life, as the demons of her past gradually took possession of her and she began to suffer from survivor's guilt. In her old age she would talk about nothing but her youth and her parents.

In 2005, after breaking her hip and shoulder in a fall, she was admitted to the Jewish care home Beth Shalom, where she spent the rest of her days. She died on 11th June 2007. A few days later she was buried in accordance with Jewish rites at the Jewish cemetery of Muiderberg.

Michaelis always struggled with her writing, and yet early in her life she said in her journal: 'I am so glad I can create poems, for it is the best feeling in the world when you are finally released from the tension and pressure of unexpressed words.' During the war she wrote: 'At least I have something that no one can take away from me.' In an interview she once said: I seem to have been blessed with a kind of animal vitality that makes me sing against the wind, so to speak.'

Her first collection, which Michaelis herself later felt was too derivative, deployed traditional forms and metres. Influences of other poets are clearly detectable in this early work: there are elements of Vasalis, whose emotionally charged poems tend to focus on the fleeting nature of life, and there are echoes of Marsman's fairly romantic and highly visual poetry.

By the time Michaelis' second collection appeared, she had let go of traditional forms and heavily poetic diction, partly under the influence of De Vijftigers (The Fifties' movement), a group of poets who rejected traditional forms and lyrical ease in favour of greater freedom and experimentation. But unlike the poetry of that movement, with its associative sounds and hermetic tendencies, her highly personal work uses direct, sober and pared-down language. In an interview she explained: 'I didn't go as far as the Fifties poets, who wanted to "sing the word free of its meaning."' However, letting go of rhyming poetry was not an easy process for her: 'When you work without strict forms, you need to discover the right form for each separate poem, and that takes time.'

It annoyed Michaelis that people assumed all her love poems

were about Reve, and she once said: 'I never made my talent subordinate to his; it was too strong for that. Poetry, for me, was a way of life, and nothing was going to stop me from writing. I am too stubborn for that.'

Much has been written about Michaelis. In an article on Michaelis' work and life, Kester Freriks writes: 'her poetry harmoniously combines big themes like death, guilt, disillusionment and love with a consciously modest, personal style. Her first collection portrays the experiences of a young woman growing up during the Occupation, and many of these poems end with a separation or a farewell, thus sharpening the sense of sadness and loneliness. Her later work explores similar themes, but in a more colloquial, anecdotal fashion.'

In his introduction to his own selection of her poetry, the Dutch novelist J.J. Voskuil emphasises the poignancy of her love poems, with their passionate, sometimes imploring Old-Testament tone, as in the poem 'Abandoned'. He feels Michaelis is at her best in her more intimate poems, which lend much of their power from their direct, sober language. He argues that, in her most melancholy, restless poems, there is an inner onlooker who stands back.

Critic Jan van der Vegt observes that Michaelis' poetry is not governed by passive resignation, but that she keeps opening the door to happiness, even if she is wary of having too many illusions, as her collection *Wegdraven naar een nieuw Utopia* ('Rushing Headlong towards a New Utopia', 1971) indicates in its very title. The collection contains strong images of regeneration, as in the poem 'Not the Chord Stretched to', where 'the grass... lifts itself up after the rain'.

Wies Roosenschoon, in an article in the journal *Tirade*, argues that her early poetry, which he places in the neo-romantic tradition, makes way for a clearer, cooler tone in her later work. The frequently used setting of a house or a room broadens to include street, beach and city, and as the perspective widens, the poetry becomes more affirmative and engaged. He also points out the subtle ways in which her later poetry tends to suggest that memory and imagination can both complement and exclude each other, and how reality must lie somewhere in between. As an example he quotes the poem 'Three Floors up in the Centre', in which present and past fuse and at once contradict each other and are reconciled.

Michaelis' work has not been widely translated yet. There has been one earlier English collection, *Against the Wind*, translated by Manfred Wolf and Paul Vincent, and a German collection. There are currently plans afoot for an English translation of her war diaries.

In translating her work, I have tried to reflect the musicality of the early poems, and the natural rhythmic ease of the later, more colloquial free verse. In my diction I have tended to avoid abstract, Latinate words as much as possible and attempted to preserve the unadorned quality of the originals.

I have chosen what I felt were the strongest poems from the different collections, although I have included some less intense, whimsical poems, such as 'Philosophising Brilliantly' and the poem about her cat, 'With Her Egyptian Eyes', to show a more light-hearted aspect of her work. I have selected a limited number of poems from her heavily romantic and at times sentimental first collection, such as the haunting 'Ghetto Children' and 'Farewell to Amsterdam'. I have, however, translated just a few of the more emphatically romantic early poems, such as 'Children's Corner', which is saved by its sardonic ending, thus foreshadowing the later Michaelis: 'Then the piano closes with a smack/and in the sober light of day I feel/all grown-up – and I know there's no road back.'

What drew me to Michaelis was her understated, direct way of expressing loss and trauma, and her grim honesty; dark as many of her poems are, they never become maudlin. A note of resilience at times undercuts the melancholy, as in the poem 'This evening I learnt/that the moon isn't round', which ends with the lines: 'I caught myself/harbouring the same stubbornness/with which I/honour other/dented illusions'. One posthumously published early poem that Michaelis was fond of, as she felt it summed up much of her attitude to life, expresses a similar resilience: 'I will have nothing or I'll have it all./I refuse to live somewhere in between.'

Michaelis's poetry is often punctuated by striking imagery, usually arising from an urban setting, where 'elongated clouds/ descend on the houses like panthers'; 'The wind theatrically yanks/the window wide open' or 'Day stretches its zebra's neck/towards a copper sun'. Her imagery is not metaphysical, it doesn't operate in an outward-bound fashion, but instead tends to reflect an inner state or a (claustrophobic) feeling.

Michaelis' analytical love poems often evoke the tensions in a relationship, homing in on the nature of a conflict ('You: a deposed tyrant... And I: your scoffing court jester') or on tentative moments of equilibrium or intimacy ('Through a swamp of hope/and despair we wade/towards each other wearily'). Some of the love poems, contained and paradoxical as they are, capture moments of great tenderness, such as 'Stretched out on Your Back', where the speaker longs to be 'softer than spume/and yet strong as resin/so I can cover you, shield you/from the needle-sharp teeth/of the night and the blight/that threaten you.'

Despite the wary note of some of Michaelis' poetry, with its sense that life inevitably brings loss and disillusionment, she nevertheless embraces the individual experience, in which the overriding logic is that of the emotions. Michaelis' range is not vast, and her vision not infused with infinite variety and invention, and yet there is a toughness, an ability to re-inhabit an experience without sentimentality or self-pity, that lends her short, focused poems a curious strength.

Judith Wilkinson

Short Prelude (1949)

THE SUNKEN CATHEDRAL
Debussy

Echoes awaken, murky and dampened,
like bells ringing in cities of the dead.
Somewhere in the depths of me, unfathomed,
the ghosts of the past begin to rear their heads.

The dreams I never dreamt to their conclusion
and the contours of an ancient tale
converge into the shape of a cathedral
rising up before me: an illusion
straight from the drowned Land of Forgetfulness,
enveloped by the pale light of memory,
an otherworldy light enticing me,
the smile of what was once lost...

O Time, relentless metronome!
The last notes sound – I'd hold them if I could –
and then the image that rose like a dream
sinks back into the depths again, for good.

CHILDREN'S CORNER
For father

Two hands over the keys, slender and swift,
bringing to life a romance of their own,
distilling music dreamlike and adrift,
so tender it would soften hearts of stone.
It is a dream in which my heart expands:
I'm spirited away by Debussy,
enchanted by the dance of ivory,
and all at once I'm back in children's land,
where puppets serenade you in the moonshine,
where shepherds slumber, garlanded with flowers,
and lovestruck snow embraces mossy bowers.
Here, melancholy and humour are entwined.
An acrobatic teddybear does cartwheels.
Then the piano closes with a smack
and in the sober light of day I feel
all grown-up – and I know there's no road back.

GHETTO CHILDREN
Amsterdam, 1942

Carefree and high-spirited their play,
malnourished as they are, their fingers blue,
they dart about the ghetto's alleyways,
not knowing what their folk are going through.

They laugh, shout, bicker and get into scraps –
sheer love of life makes them look for trouble.
Even here, power falls into the fittest laps
and no one minds enough to prick the bubble.

Where adults gather, talking in muffled tones,
muttering their sorrows, anxious and depressed,
their children's laughter bounces off the stones,
undamaged as they are, their minds at rest.

They're given free reign, their doubts are put to bed,
their ghetto is an earthly paradise,
despite the sword that hangs above their heads,
reflected in the deep pools of their eyes.

FAREWELL TO AMSTERDAM

The tram at Central screeches to a halt.
As we get out, I feel the city's call.
Thank God: I'm sentimental after all.
A civil sun is hiding in its vault.

Once more my heavy eyes flutter
like weary birds carried by the evening wind
across the elegant, stone labyrinth
of domes, church spires, gables and gutters
serrating a pale sky, across whose plain
grey, fraying shreds of cloud are drifting along.

How long will I be gone?
Perhaps I will return again one day.
But who can say...

As I escape into the station hall,
a drop falls on my cheek: it is the rain.

Water Out of the Rock (1957)

The sky has the pallor
of mysterious, unborn life
that is everywhere and nowhere,
imperceptibly entangled
in a fine web of branches full of longing.
In expectant water it opens its eyes,
smiling in the shadowless light,
inhaling the gentle wind.
And along the housefronts,
high above the roofs,
the dream of a blessed season rises:
a hopeful, hesitant budding
that will break out in riotous blossoms
before bearing fruit tenderly, thoughtfully.
If all this is not for you,
you will roam the streets like an empty shell,
your heart numb and hostile,
reluctant to greet the spring.

This is the hour when I don't want to be alone.
Shakily the sun scrawls
orange signs on white walls –
a horror I can't fathom.
Outside, elongated clouds
descend on the houses like panthers.
Trails of blood float on the water
and in the room where I'm standing, alone,
a leaden twilight pushes in silently
like doom.
The dry ticking of the clock
grows more and more emphatic,
like the pecking of a beak
on the yellow, glass wall of the West
that I'll be headed for one day,
unwillingly, with limbs like lead.

Moving through time, we carefully
carry eggshells filled to the brim
with tears.

In the mirrors of our eyes
the world rises desolately.
We have been everywhere.
We return nowhere.

Weighed down by memories
we bend towards the earth.
Unknowing and unwise
we wither and leave no trace.

You took the blood-red route
of my longing
to reach me.

Along the road that seemed impassable
you take me
to a hidden source.
My hand in yours, I walk blindly,
trembling
with impatience and fear.

If you let go of me now
I'll stumble.
Then the wind will rise up from the desert
and the sand will close above me
like water.

This evening when I'd fled
to the window to escape the empty room
that resented your absence,
your warmth flooded me
with sudden force.

Motionlessly content, the trees
leaned against the sky.
A replete silence
hovered over the earth.

Then the first raindrops fell
slowly and solemnly
and tears suddenly welled
from my eyes, warm and
redemptive as the water
Moses struck from the rocks.

Beyond each other's reach
we wake up at the same hour
as if by appointment.

Blue-green morning light
flows out across the city.
Roused by the din of triumphant birds,
the day that will betray us all over again
approaches.

Through a swamp of hope
and despair we wade
towards each other wearily:
two shadows embracing
above the place where we drowned.

Beneath restless clouds
the wind slunk past
like an animal with no lair.

You hid your face against my neck
as if there were no more hope
of shelter for our happiness,
which is as restless as the clouds
and homeless as the wind.

You give me water
when I'm thirsty
and bread to still my hunger,
but in my mouth
the water becomes bitter
and the bread is like grit
between my teeth.

I bite the hand
that caresses me,
your warmth
I let go to waste.

And yet you are the one
I'm looking for. Therefore
you must kill me.

Listening to the music
we used to hear together,
I tug at my sadness
the way a dog tugs at its chain.

Violins and flutes weave
a silver web
over an abyss
before silence
shuts me in again.

Under its frosted bell-jar
the soundless struggle
between hope and despair
breaks out again
over the no man's land
of my life.

Cold and infertile
like the West:
a crystal ball, filled
with wintry light.

But when the cloud
of a memory
drifts in imperceptibly
and the thaw sets in,
a red-hot spiral of pain
shoots through me.

Sleepless in the cavern
of the night.

All roads to you
rolled up into a black
inextricable tangle.

Needle-sharp pain
spinning round in the groove
of a memory.

And outside the gentle
unintelligible murmuring of
the spring rain.

In October the light
is as thin as the blue
transparent skin
of a dying person.

The tree can no longer
hold on to its leaves
and the hand opens
to let go of the amulet
that has turned to ashes.

Against the imperishable sky
the white skeleton
of our love.

Against the Wind (1962)

What did you do
that put you on trial
in my dreams
before a tribunal
of die-hard partisans?

In the hollow light
their weary faces
bend over a table
with the evidence:
copper coins
and a charred piece of paper,
curling at the edges.

What did you do
to make me wrap my arms
round you in vain,
crying: he is no traitor!

In the window with no view
a soldier appears,
pointing his rifle.

What did you do
to yourself?

You: a deposed tyrant,
restlessly milling around
in your comfortable house
among your books and paintings
and the silent life
of plants.

And I: your scoffing court jester,
summoned for your entertainment,
caressed and rebuked
because I won't submit
to your reign – your fiction.

Occasionally the two of us listen
to the wind at the window
as it calls us with the voice
of the cosmos.

How much longer
will the fear in your eyes
keep us imprisoned?

Abandoned
in an uninhabitable world
jangling with colours
and sounds,
where the day is too bright
and no night dark enough
to calm
the hidden tumult.

In every street, in every room
I keep searching for you.
Among innumerable people
I cannot find you anywhere.

Deliver me
from this void.
Let me enter the earth
that covers you.
I want to sleep close to you
and turn to dust.

Underwater
I engrave your name
in the granite riverbed
where I flow.

Between the weeds
of the past
fish flash by
like knives.

From now on I can meet you
only in the depths:
my warm counter-flow,
my love.

What is certain
is that you're dead.
But what is dead?

Invisibly
you meet me
on my arduous journey
across the moonscape
of time.

Inaudibly
your voice penetrates
my most secret
listening post.

You who know all my ways,
who have deciphered and read me,
stay with me
invisibly, inaudibly
and lead me across the threshold
of death.

Slowly I move on
across windless plains.
There's nothing left to fear,
nothing to expect.

Footsteps are little more
than faint sounds in the fog.
I vaguely register
unfamiliar voices.
Why should I answer?

Living blindly,
in the footsteps of your death,
I seem to be moving
away from your grave, on the road
to my own.

Years later
one clear afternoon
full of sober sounds
and the hustle and bustle in a house
that never knew you,
I suddenly remember
how gentle your eyes would become
when you looked at me.

And for a moment you appear before me,
unmistakably you, coming across unexpectedly
from timelessness.
So gentle are your eyes
that they reconcile me
with your departure, swifter,
more unexpected than your arrival.

Give me the elusive oasis,
the mirage shimmering
above the hot sands
of the desert,
let me come face to face
with the impassive sphinx
who won't have his secret
wrested from him,
let me be buried under a pyramid
of self-deception
rather than be trapped in the peace
of a valley with no vistas,
where life quietly
trickles towards death.

With her Egyptian eyes –
night-blue pupils
set in luminous green –
the cat eyes me.
She doesn't understand me at all,
but she is soft
and warm under her coat
of good faith.

Somewhere in this city
I am bound to find you.

Of all the people
you run into
there is perhaps not one
who looks for you as longingly
as I do.

Even in my dreams
you hide away.
Unfindable, withdrawn,
you won't so much as glance at me
or send me a sign.

That's how a god punishes
the one who dares to
come too close.

The night is lighter
or darker
than it was then.

Why won't memory
let go of its loot
when the well has been poisoned,
the dream collapsed?

The only refuge
is sleep. Falling back
into the ocean of the unborn
and drowning.

To be worry-free
and not fret
about the morning –
be it lighter
or darker
than it was then.

In an unguarded moment,
yearning, I stole in
and have lost my way inside you.

A barbaric landscape
bears the sparse signs
of your presence:
the defoliated tree
that casts no shadow,
the blackened shrubbery,
the dried-up creek
between the rocks
and deep beneath the grey
thirsty crust of the earth
the muffled rushing
of murmuring water
that can find no way out.

Ominously low
the yellow sun hangs
above the roofs.
Trees wring their branches
as the wind rises.

Fear presses an ice-cold
hand in my neck. Where
are you? What is
happening to you?

I'd like to be
softer than spume
and yet strong as resin
so I can cover you, shield you
from the needle-sharp teeth
of the night and the blight
that threaten you.

If it isn't ours
I don't want it, this spring
with its spring tide of light,
its splash of colours.

The bronze clouds, luxuriantly
stacked against flaming blue,
the trees flecked with the
finest green, motionless
in the dove-grey evening,
and the opal smile of
world-embracing rainbows
are wasted
on me solo.

Thinking of how we used to be together
and might be again some day,
I see thirsty green
against a thundery sky.

A tense calm between absence
and abundance. Unbearably
heightened desire.

Tree tops stretch towards
the slanting heavens.

Breathtaking balance
before space tilts
and the rain falls.

Submerged
in the tidal wave of an embrace,
I hear your voice in my ear,
whispering imploringly:
forget about later.

A shrouded omen
that makes me shiver fleetingly
against the warmth of
your body, your naked skin.

Footsteps coming down the stairs.
Silence descends like a spider
from the attic. The room
is filled with grey threads.
Between the walls
antiquated light lingers.

The currency of the here
and now converted
into the notes
of memory.

Taste me
like bread. Drink me,
breathe me in.

The inside of your skin
I'll kiss, your bones
I'll warm. Your heart
that beats against your ribs
like a caged bird
I'll caress more gently than
light brushing the treetops.

Since there is much that I
no longer care about,
let me be ingrained in you
and not live outside you.

Sad
as the light
of the introverted moon
behind nocturnal cloud-hedges
and just as unapproachable.

In the leafless light
of a windless autumn day
the elderly
look touchingly beautiful.

Because they've
given up the struggle
with decay and no longer
fear mirrors, they've grown
fragile and transparent
as spun glass, with the soft,
mysterious glow of silver.

Disconcertingly close-to-the-bone,
the white face
of day, skulking
in a collar of clouds.
The dark wide-open eye
of a puddle of rain. The bird
that sings in defiance of the wind,
swaying as the light
makes its last stand.

Unexpected (1966)

Tantalising uncertainty,
breeding ground for fabulous
misunderstandings, dazzling
weeds of doubt
to which hope clings
until death.

Minutes spread
into years
in the dead-straight
empty street
where I traipse after myself
reluctantly.

Trapped between
two rows of houses
the sun awaits its demise.

It's terrible.
Everything starts afresh
as if nothing happened.

In thorny branches
the racket of birds.
Squeaking and screeching,
spring sets in. The wind
plucks untuned chords
of hope and delusion.

Nothing
happened. Everything
starts afresh. It's
terrible.

Intimacy:
a body awesome
in its naked vulnerability,
keeper of a buried
and shy secret
that exposes itself – just for an instant.

But also
our speechless despair
when in the evening light the room
began to levitate all by itself
and stayed suspended in space
with no connection to the world
of trains, news reports,
people sitting down at table.

As if we had been tried and
found wanting
for life at ground level.

When the inexpressible
had revealed itself
in the speechless language of two
bodies rounded into one,
all that remained was peace
and well-being. Now, you said,
we lie in God's hand.
And so we did, but
it couldn't stay that way.

Midnight. Moon
over spring trees.
Dutch gables in the light
of streetlamps.
The city domesticated into
a reassuring picture
that includes me –
even though my head is
full of centrifugal shards
that no one can see.

Some days I see gems,
on others they're bits of scrap.
The light falls as it chooses.
But whether it's morning or evening,
yesterday or the day after tomorrow,
everything is still in pieces.

The racket of an alarm clock
tears me pitilessly from my warm
cocoon of sheets and blankets
into the day.

The room looks surprisingly
lived-in, with the vaguely
familiar clothes draped across a chair.

When I turn round
a naked man is perched on the edge
of my bed. Seeing his smile
I think to myself:
the woman who lives here
is to be envied.

The I who
loses and recovers herself
in your embrace is not
the one who walks out
of your life with leaden feet
nor the one who
convinces herself that you
were never here at all.

All three locked
inside my skin, they have
come to blows in a war
of life or death.

Love rolled away
to the other end
of the world. Faith
smothered in the mud
of questions and quandaries.
Even hope has scrambled off
betrayed – and yet
there's enough left not to want to die
and from time to time
to embrace its scarcity
as eagerly as I once embraced
its abundance.

Over the years
a great deal has to be thrown out.
The notion, for instance,
that happiness is mild and enduring,
something like a southern climate
instead of a bolt of lightning
that leaves scars
cherished a lifetime.

On a country road –
with not a soul about, only
a few sleeping ducks tucked away
in the grass, while the lights
of scattered farms
compete with the evening star –
peace brushes my eyes.

But inside me
homesickness restlessly
hunts for the remnants of an earlier
life when somebody's arms
carried me back
to the silence of before
the beginning, which suddenly
turned into the silence
of after the end.

The Rock of Gibraltar (1969)

This evening I learnt
that the moon isn't round
but pear-shaped,
with at least two
bulges, maybe
even three. Later,
when I looked out,
a round, incandescent
disc climbed up
above the roofs
and I caught myself
harbouring the same
stubbornness with which I
honour other
dented illusions.

In the dead of night
the wind theatrically yanks
the window wide open.

On moonlit roofs
beneath shredded clouds
man-sized angular insects
wobble about quietly on one leg.
A peculiar detail
from the delusional brain
of the giant muddle-head
that invented me as well.

It's an ordinary day. The sun
is shining on a buzzing city.

Suddenly
silence falls like a shot.
A swarm of projectiles
passes over, exploding
soundlessly. Ash-coloured light
descends, invading
the houses, deadly. Nobody
tries to get away: there
is no escape –

Waking up sweating
I hear a dove cooing
closeby. The sun is shining
over a buzzing city.
It's an ordinary day.

Three floors up in the heart
of Amsterdam I recall
the Rock of Gibraltar,
a sparkling pin cushion
lifted up by the sea
towards low-hanging stars
while I recalled
the image of a bulge
rising from a blue plain
looked at frequently by a child
filled with vague thoughts of a future
that is now the past.

Irretrievably buried
beneath the sand of two summers
and snowed under in three winters.

But when I saw the photo in a newspaper
of a guerrilla fighter murdered
in South America, lying on his back,
eyes half closed, strangely relaxed,
his shirt pulled up, revealing his smooth
body naked to the waist,
I felt something shift inside me,
as if another body inside mine
moved unexpectedly, raised its eyes
briefly, before closing them slowly again.

Sparrows twittering.
Water shivering lasciviously
in the wind.
A suspicion of green
steals up on the trees
while I am stalked by
visions of charred bodies
among smoking rubble.

In the light
of the cloud-swept
ice-blue evening sky, the sun
just down, the stars not out yet,
it's irrelevant
how I'm feeling, who I
sleep with and whether
I'll still be here tomorrow.
In this sober, frosty light
I'm no more than an easily-removed
speck of dust
in the lens of a candid camera.

The suppressed glow
of red and blue glass
smouldering in the twilight
of a smoky-grey winter's day.

I noticed it in passing
when I was barely five years old
as I was led by the hand
through the Rijksmuseum
by a purposeful adult.

Late in the afternoon,
from a sky that still holds
warmth and sunlight
in folds of grey velvet,
it suddenly starts raining.
The wind turns at lightning speed,
cold tumbles into the room.
I get up to close the window.
The ways of low-pressure areas
are as inscrutable
as those of fate.

Distant lightning
drives orange cracks
into a concrete sky.
An oppressive ceiling
that refuses to break open.
The firmament growls, tormented,
from the bedrock of my heart.

The body
that contents itself with
another body
since the one
became unavailable
must from time to time
turn a blind eye
to its own consciousness
as it escapes to a remote
half-overgrown
corner of memory
and so betrays
the betrayal.

A hilltop under majestic
clouds. The view friendly enough.
Red-tiled roofs between
summery trees, dark-blue
sun-splashed water flowing
towards forests on the horizon.
And there was someone beside me. All
the conditions for an idyllic
time together seemed to have been met
when I was struck by a feeling I used to have
during the war (no home, just a
roof over my head, outlawed in the polder)
and I was reduced to my true
proportions: a helpless creature
with no name, no significance,
who could be snatched from the earth
and crushed at any moment. Of course
nothing of the kind happened.
Unharmed and in the best of moods
we walked down the hill. But
my feeling could not be explained,
let alone understood.

An elongated factory
full of tubing and scaffolding and soft machinery,
where work goes on day and night
in utter darkness.

Nothing is more mine
than this under-the-skin round-the-clock industry,
but when I think about it
I become a hollow word.

I was about three years old
when, one autumn evening,
standing at the window looking out,
my nose for the first time
sticking out above the windowsill,
I discovered
a house was being built
opposite ours. I announced
with great conviction:
they will take it away again in the summer.
My mother, who had no say in the matter,
laughed. Towards the end of
the Second World War when my parents
had already been gassed, the Germans
set fire to that house. After the liberation
it was rebuilt. It still stands there today
and I have recurring dreams
about concrete and brick buildings
that utterly erase
a promising view.

Philosophising brilliantly
about life, I
overcook the potatoes.
Unmistakable proof
of emancipation.

A body trusted and familiar
from many other nights,
naked and relaxed,
looking for mine in its sleep.
A hand fleetingly
caresses my hip. I feel
wonderfully privileged
and terribly vulnerable.

Rushing Headlong Towards A New Utopia (1971)

Reaching the bars of her cage,
the beautiful dishevelled she-wolf
interrupts her restless pacing.
With baited breath
I try to meet her gaze.
She looks straight through me
with her pale, translucent eyes
that remind me of yours
when, halfway through a sentence,
you stop and stare ahead blankly.
Sad. Despairing. Unapproachable.

Five o'clock on a Saturday afternoon.
From breaking clouds
a scrap of light escapes.
The world smells of spring.
In the pub across the street,
just as the streetlights go on,
the jukebox starts blasting out music:
'For the times they are a-changing'
Bob Dylan sings, and I know
winter is coming.

A day out had brought us
to the sea. Between
all the other people we stood
on a cramped beach.
Near us dark clumps of stalactite
enveloped a patch of
colourless, corrugated metal.

It looked nothing like the sea
near Estepona that summer afternoon
years ago
lazily licking the brown sand,
stretching out under a lilac sky
and open in all directions,
although that was the first scene
I thought of as I woke up with the vague
feeling I'd forfeited something.

Stretched out on your back
with your feet in the present
and your head connected to
some irretrievably distant
past it is no wonder
the tension threatens to break you
every night.
But that you find the strength
every morning afresh
to raise yourself and get out of bed
leaves me awestruck.

What it would have been like
if I hadn't known you, except perhaps
by hearsay or appearance –
easier, I suppose:
not those constant wasp-stings
of fear and doubt. Nor
those islands of tropical bliss
in a polar sea of discontent.

Five identical tower blocks
on a bare plain
reflect the evening sun.
A battle array of scarlet signs
rising steeply into nothingness.
The train in which we sit
rushes past anxiously,
as if to spare us the terrible beauty
of inescapable doom.

Statements
may be swept off the table,
pushed away, smothered
in comforting embraces.
And yet they
have the longest life
and the last word.

Not the chord stretched to
breaking point nor the watch spring
wound up too far
nor the overheated glass,
but the grass that
lifts itself up after the rain, the fire
under the embers, Bouvard
and Pécuchet who, when all other
plans have failed spectacularly,
even suicide, watch the snow
melt, breathe in the scents of spring
and rush headlong
towards a new utopia.

Faces in a haze
of cigarette smoke. Voices
carefully weaving a conversation.
Nothing touches me, there's nobody
to be afraid of – except for
one whom my eyes avoid
by escaping to the window.

From a gap between roofs
and house fronts, the church tower
of the Zuiderkerk boldly reaches
into the serene, white-flocked
spring air. The weathercock
sparkles gloriously in the evening sun
as if, at the last moment,
it wants to convert me to the faith
in Gorter's golden-blue days
that are now. Now.

Chattering away and full of purpose
we walked through the evening.
Above the baroque hodgepodge
of beautiful and ugly houses,
wild wintry clouds caught
the last light on their crests.
Early green shivered in the wind,
just as we did as we paused briefly
on the bridge and looked out across
the Amstel in silence.
The summer seemed endlessly far away
and tangibly close.

When, with light fingertips,
you read me like Braille,
carefully and lovingly,
lions and tigers laid their
heads on their paws
and slept, snakes coiled
themselves up and even the scorpion
retired. Liberated,
I drew breath, I felt
your heart beating against mine
and inside me all grew still
as in the empty church just
before the organ
raises its triumphant voice.

He who closes his curtains
and lights candles
in broad daylight,
he who tries to stop time
for the sake of a smile, a gesture,
and envies the mediaeval lovers
(who, as the legend goes,
turned to stone in each other's arms),
will lose what he possesses
and more.

Your face unrecognisably
tender and at the same time
more familiar than my own
as it looks at me uncertainly
in the mirror each day.
Through the mist of evaporated
years the promise of you appears
in a flash, unmistakeable.
With your arms round me
it's as if the circle
of my life is complete.
Perhaps the miracle
touched me, perhaps
I am saved.

A morning
like any other.
The cool light
impassive, but without
the old brusqueness.
The day has shed
its thorns, since the night
was gentle and dark,
since a gesture
defeated our words
and warmth could flow unhampered, in long
waves of release, since
peace – for years a fugitive –
allowed itself to be found at last,
blindfold.

Poems Published Posthumously

How charmingly
the city stretches out
in the peachy glow
of a low sun.
Between her stone pleats
the downy blue-grey
of the newborn evening,
and all around her
a green, serene universe
shrinking in its tentacles.

The white, brazen stare
of mercury lamps above an empty
asphalt road. Dark houses
against a dark sky
repeating themselves in dark water.

Between bone-dry shrubs
the December wind crouches.

A unique place for anyone
venturing to disappear unseen,
bicycle and all,
into the Styx.

Slowly but surely
day stretches its zebra's neck
towards a copper sun.
Wind ruffles the wet
green hair of city parks,
unrolls a stark blue flag
over the roofs. Whoever sees this
has survived the night,
like it or not.

Suddenly, from somewhere
high up, a shower of shot is fired
at the city.
Like a colossal, flaming spider
the sun eases itself
straight down from a cloud,
setting fire to the west.
On the other side a rainbow appears
with Old Testament authority.
Glows. Fades
without having touched the earth.

As dusk was setting in
I looked out and saw
an unfamiliar white house in the distance
between familiar trees.
My gaze greeted the house, surprised,
as if it were an outpost of some peerless world
that would one day open for me.
The next evening the house
had disappeared. No matter how I looked for it,
in the twilight or during the day,
it didn't reappear.
A premature promise, withdrawn
prematurely. During the last decades
it has kept rising up in me from time to time:
a white house between distant trees.
Unfindable. Otherworldly.

I don't want to be grateful and make do
with the crumbs of a comfortable fate.
I won't bow my head under the weight
of duty, pious prayers that don't ring true.

I will have nothing or I'll have it all.
I refuse to live somewhere in between.
If the path ahead is narrow, let me fall –
and I will plumb the depths of a ravine.

The smoke of my cigarette
spirals upwards towards to the stars.
Despair has infected my heart,
my memories block the path

that leads to Oblivion –
and how I long to forget…
Will I ever be freed
from what I never possessed?

That evening I waited for a long while
before I heard your footstep on the stairs.
With every dying stroke of the clock
my fear grew like a wild animal
about to fly at me
if the last hope were to escape me.
It took forever – then you were there in the doorway,
a stranger, almost an enemy;
the question I hardly dared ask
died on my lips when I saw
how timidly your eyes avoided mine,
afraid to show the burning joy
whose untamable fire
would scorch the remnants of my own
because I had no part in it.

Deep into the evening
hundreds of starlings
are wide awake in their sleep-trees
along the busy canal.
With every sudden
explosion of sound they
start shouting.
Their shrill protests
shatter the hourglass
of the night, lending a voice
to the mute despair
of troubled souls
who lie sleepless
in the dark.

Indestructible. A word
like a pennant
waving beneath storm clouds.
They used to say that
about my mother. Many years
younger than I am now, she wrote to me
from a camp on the rural moorland
near the village of Westerbork
in a letter smuggled out:
'it's quite doable here.'
My unworldly, lovable father,
ripped from his piano,
had added: 'Don't worry.
We'll meet again soon.'
By the time I read those lines ten days later,
my parents, along with hundreds of others,
had been transported in overcrowded, blacked-out
cattle trains right across Germany to Sobibor,
where they were gassed on arrival.
This happened in March 1943.
No matter for poetry.

The night after I learnt
that someone I loved more than
myself had died in an accident,
he returned to me in my sleep.
He was in a wheelchair,
wrapped in a blanket covering
all of him except his head.
I was three steps away from him.
When I tried to come closer
something invisible stopped me.
He smiled at me
as if wanting to comfort me.
A dream that has survived reality
by dozens of years.

A ruinous wind
assaults the trees. Whirling leaves
clutch their branches in vain.
Clouds are swept together
and shoved under the horizon.
Soon the whimsical stars
will jump into their
fixed lines.
I will witness them, losing myself
in what lies behind me
so as not to look ahead
to where the path grows narrow
and breaks off.

Today and yesterday
and later merge
in the night's groundwater.
Above gardens and the backs of houses
a wide-open ochre eye
watches in the darkness
where nothing moves. Deep inside me
not a thought, not a feeling stirs.
Unreal equilibrium
without a hint of peace.

NOTES

'Farewell to Amsterdam', p. 14: this poem was written during the war, shortly after Michaelis had to leave Amsterdam to go into hiding.

'Faces in a haze', p. 95: 'Gorter's golden-blue days' this refers to Herman Gorter's poem 'Pan', in which he writes of a socialist Utopia, a 'golden-blue time'.